"The benefits of this guide are similar to the benefits of the creed that provides its structure: a strong focus on Christology and the Trinity. A basic understanding of the Father, the Son, and the Spirit are foundational for the Christian life, and this guide provides that foundation for new believers."

Paul Hoskins
Associate Professor of New Testament
Southwestern Baptist Theological Seminary

"*Grounded in the Faith* is a treasure trove of Scripture and concise theology arranged for the new believer and a mentor to explore together. I will be distributing this easily accessible text to all our new members, and await rich, transformative conversations to unfold!"

Rev. Dr. Case Thorp
Senior Associate Pastor for Evangelism
First Presbyterian Church of Orlando, FL

Ministry and Discipleship Guides

Grounded in the Faith: A Guide for New Disciples Based on the Apostles' Creed, by Todd A. Scacewater
Internalizing the Faith: A Pilgrim's Catechism, by J. Brandon Burks
Living the Faith: Upward, Inward, Outward, and Onward, by Brian Albert

Grounded in the Faith

A Guide for New Disciples
Based on the Apostles' Creed

Grounded in the Faith

A Guide for New Disciples
Based on the Apostles' Creed

Todd A. Scacewater

Fontes Press

Grounded in the Faith:
A Guide for New Disciples Based on the Apostles' Creed

1st ed. copyright © 2017 by Todd A. Scacewater

Revised ed. copyright © 2019 by Todd A. Scacewater

ISBN-13: 978-1-948048-18-7 (paperback)
ISBN-13: 978-1-948048-19-4 (hardback)

Scripture quotations are from the ESV® Bible (The Holy Bible, English Standard Version®), copyright © 2001 by Crossway, a publishing ministry of Good News Publishers. Used by permission. All rights reserved.

All rights reserved. No part of this publication may be reproduced, stored in a retrieval system, or transmitted in any form or by any means—electronic, mechanical, photocopy, recording, or any other—except for brief quotations in printed reviews, without the prior permission of the publisher.

FONTES PRESS
DALLAS, TX

www.fontespress.com

To my wife, Dezi, who shares and fuels my
passion for discipleship and devotion to Christ.

Contents

Preface xi

Part 1: God the Father

Session 1	Introduction: The Ancient Christian Confession 1	
Session 2	I Believe 9	
Session 3	God the Father Almighty, Creator of Heaven and Earth 13	

Part 2: Jesus Christ

Session 4	Jesus Christ, His Only Son, Our Lord 19	
Session 5	Who Was Conceived by the Holy Spirit, Born of the Virgin Mary 25	
Session 6	Suffered under Pontius Pilate 29	
Session 7	Was Crucified, Died, and Was Buried; He Descended to the Dead 33	
Session 8	On the Third Day, He Rose Again; He Ascended into Heaven, He is Sitting at the Right Hand of God the Father Almighty 39	
Session 9	From Where He is Coming to Judge the Living and the Dead 43	

Part 3: The Gifts of God

Session 10	The Holy Spirit 49	
Session 11	The Holy Universal Church, the Communion of Saints 53	
Session 12	The Forgiveness of Sins, the Resurrection of the Body, and the Life Everlasting 57	
Next Steps	Beginning to Grow in the Faith 61	

Preface

This work is intended for pastors, elders, church leaders, and laymen to use to disciple new believers. When a person repents, trusts in Christ, and begins following him, we must disciple them (Matthew 28:18–20). Discipleship includes teaching the faith and modeling it with our lives, which involves an ongoing relationship with God and with those whom we are discipling.

This guide serves as a crash course on the basic tenets of the Christian faith. Ministers, leaders, or capable laypersons can work through this guide with new believers to ensure that they understand the faith to which they have committed themselves. The time spent together in this guide will also form the basis for an ongoing spiritual mentorship.

The content is intentionally aimed at the intellect, although content and discussion questions do invite the reader to reflect on whether they have truly been saved. The reason for omitting life-application content and discussion questions is to ensure that this guide has a singular, measurable objective: to confirm that new believers actually understand the faith they claim to hold. Leaders can move toward practical application if they wish, given their own setting and abilities. But the guide is written so that each user will achieve the same goal of comprehending the basics of the faith, which should create a firm foundation on which to grow in the faith. The final chapter provides the user with "next steps," including the various ways in which we grow in our faith and some resources to set them in the right direction.

Session 1

Introduction:
The Ancient Christian Confession

"If you confess with your mouth that Jesus is Lord and believe in your heart that God raised him from the dead, you will be saved" (Romans 10:9).

When we repent of our sin and trust in Christ for salvation, we make a confession—that is, we make a public declaration that we believe something. According to Romans 10:9, that confession is that "Jesus is Lord." But simply speaking the words "Jesus is Lord" as a magical formula does not save us. We must understand the meaning of this confession so that the content of our faith is true. This guide for new disciples aims to help the reader understand the meaning of the confession "Jesus is Lord" by teaching the basics of the biblical story from the creation of the world to the final judgment when Jesus returns. Only within this broad story that God gives us in his Word can we understand the true meaning of "Jesus is Lord."

Since the early days of the church, its leaders have wanted to ensure that new disciples understood the faith they proclaimed. Leaders would typically teach these new disciples the basics of the Christian faith to prepare them for baptism. While there was no formal document that all churches used, there were similar informal "creeds" (statements of belief) that we find scattered throughout the writings of church leaders from as early as the second century. By AD 390, these informal creeds from different regions had become so similar that one church leader named the entire tradition "the Apostles' Creed." This title reflects the (erroneous) ancient belief that the creed was written by the apostles after Jesus' resurrection and before they dispersed to preach the gospel.[1] But the title is appropriate enough, since the language and teaching of the creed is drawn directly from the teaching of the apostles as recorded in the New Testament.

By around AD 400, the form of the Apostles' Creed as it was found in churches around the world had essentially the same teaching, with very minor differences in wording. The final form of the Apostles' Creed that churches around the world recite today was solidified by around AD 700.[2]

---

[1] This traditional belief that the apostles wrote the creed is testified by Rufinus in the fourth century (*A Commentary on the Apostles' Creed*, trans. and annotated by J. N. D. Kelly, Ancient Christian Writers 20 [Newman Press, 1978], 29–30).

[2] See John H. Leith, ed. *Creeds of the Churches: A Reader in Christian Doctrine from the Bible to the Present*, 3rd ed.

Since church leaders have used this creed to teach new disciples for more than 1,600 years, we can be assured that it stands as a true representation of the Bible's teaching. Its use by millions of church leaders to teach new disciples also suggests it contains the most essential teachings of the faith that all new disciples should know. As one eminent church historian put it, the creed "contains all the fundamental articles of the Christian faith necessary to salvation, in the form of facts, in simple Scripture language, and in the most natural order—the order of revelation—from God and the creation down to the resurrection and life everlasting."[3] For these reasons, we will use the Apostles' Creed as our guide to the Bible's message. Our goal is to gain a broad understanding of the Bible's teaching so that we can truly comprehend the confession that leads to salvation: "Jesus is Lord."

The text of the Apostles' Creed, as churches have used it since around AD 700, reads as follows:

(Westminster John Knox, 1982), 22–25; Henry Bettenson and Chris Maunder eds., *Documents of the Christian Church*, 3rd ed. (Oxford University Press, 1999), 25–26; Philip Schaff, *The Creeds of Christendom, with a History and Critical Notes*, 6th rev. ed. (Harper & Brothers), 1:16–20.

[3] Schaff, *The Creeds of Christendom*, 1:14–15.

I believe in God, the Father almighty,
> creator of heaven and earth.
and in Jesus Christ, his only Son, our Lord,
> who was conceived by the Holy Spirit,
> born of the Virgin Mary,
> suffered under Pontius Pilate,
> was crucified, died, and was buried;
> he descended to the dead;
> on the third day, he rose again;
> he ascended into heaven,
> he is sitting at the right hand of God the Father almighty,
> from where he is coming to judge the living and the dead.
I believe in the Holy Spirit,
> the holy universal[4] Church,
> the communion of saints,
> the forgiveness of sins,
> the resurrection of the body,
> and the life everlasting.
Amen.

---

[4] This word is usually translated "catholic," which means "general" or "worldwide," not "Catholic" in the sense of the Roman Catholic Church.

Figure 1. A painting of the twelve apostles receiving inspiration from the Holy Spirit and composing the Apostles' Creed, from Somme le Roy, a moral compendium compiled in 1279 by the Dominican Friar Laurent for King Philip III of France. Available online: http://www.bl.uk/manuscripts/Viewer.aspx?ref=add_ms_54180_fs001r.

Discussion

1. Why must we understand the meaning of the confession "Jesus is Lord" in order to be truly saved?
2. If the Apostles' Creed was not actually written by the apostles, why is it still a valuable creed to study at the beginning of one's faith journey?
3. After reading the Apostles' Creed above, which parts are you interested in learning more about? Why?

Part 1

GOD THE FATHER

Session 2

I Believe

The word "creed" comes from the Latin verb *credo*, which means "I believe." The Apostles' Creed is a statement of what Christians believe. But before we can examine what we believe, we have to ask, "what is belief?" Or better, what is faith?

Scripture speaks often of faith "in Christ." The essence of faith is not simply believing in something, but placing our absolute trust in a person. "The wages of sin is death, but the free gift of God is eternal life in Christ Jesus our Lord" (Romans 6:23). By trusting in Christ as our Lord and Savior, our sins are no longer counted against us and we receive God's free gift of eternal life.[1]

Our ability to place our faith in Christ is not based on our own ability. Scripture says we were "dead in our trespasses and sins" (Ephesians 2:1; see also Colossians 2:13) before God saved us. We were "enemies" of God (Romans

---

[1] Romans 3:28; 5:1; Galatians 2:16; 3:11; 3:24.

5:10) and completely unable to save ourselves, or even to bring ourselves to believe the glorious truths of the gospel. "By grace you have been saved through faith. And this is not your own doing; it is the gift of God, not a result of works, so that no one may boast" (Ephesians 2:8–9). Salvation through faith, then, is a gift of God.

But at the same time, faith is a personal decision that is made because of the gracious work of the Holy Spirit in our hearts. It involves a personal decision to turn from the idols of our heart to the true and living God and to Christ our Savior.[2] It is also a genuine commitment that results in a new heart (Ezekiel 36:26). This commitment results in a new way of living for God rather than for sin. The Bible rejects any idea of faith that simply claims to confess Jesus as Lord without actually resulting in a new way of life. "Faith without works is dead" (see James 2:17).

Discussion

1. Read Ephesians 2:8–9. How are we saved?
2. Read Galatians 2:16. Can we be saved through our own good works?
3. Read Ezekiel 36:26–27, which describes what happens when we are saved through faith in Christ. How is a new believer's life different than before salvation?
4. How has God changed your heart since you started following Christ? How does your life look different?

---

[2] C. E. B. Cranfield, *The Apostles' Creed: A Faith to Live By* (Continuum, 2004), 8–9.

Figure 2. Possibly the oldest recognizable portrayal of Jesus, painted on the baptistery wall of a Syrian church in the early third century. It depicts Jesus healing the paralytic: "And when Jesus saw their *faith*, he said to the paralytic, 'Son, your sins are forgiven'" (Mark 2:5). The *faith* of the paralytic and his friends moved them to *trust* in Jesus for healing. Image in the public domain: https://artgallery.yale.edu/collections/objects/34498.

SESSION 3

GOD THE FATHER ALMIGHTY, CREATOR OF HEAVEN AND EARTH

The Bible begins with God the Father: "In the beginning, God created the heavens and the earth" (Genesis 1:1). God existed before everything else and has always existed. He spoke everything into existence by his word (Genesis 1:3–31). By these truths, we see that God is *Almighty*. "Our God is in the heavens; he does all that he pleases" (Psalm 115:3). As creator of the universe, he is incomparably mightier and greater than every part of creation. Jesus could even refer to the Father as "the Power" (Mark 14:62).[1]

But at the same time, God is intimately relational with his people, so that we can call him *Father*. He first described himself as a father to his chosen people Israel. As they were enslaved in Egypt, God declared to Pharaoh, "Is-

---

[1] Capitalized rightly in many modern English translations (Cranfield, *The Apostles' Creed*, 15).

rael is my firstborn son...let my son go that he may serve me" (Exodus 4:22–23). It follows that God is only "Father" to those whom he saves and adopts into his spiritual family (see Romans 8:15).

God uses this human relationship of fatherhood to signify how he relates to us. Of course, he is a *perfect* Father, and carries none of the abuses or failures of human fathers. We must judge human fathers by the perfect standard of God as our Father, rather than viewing God through the lens of our imperfect fathers. To make the mistake of viewing God in light of our human fathers would give us a drastically distorted view of who God is.

While God is the adopted Father of those whom he saves, he is also the "Father of our Lord Jesus Christ."[2] We know this fatherly relationship with his Son is eternal because Scripture says that all of creation was made "through" the Son, "and nothing that was made was made without him."[3] So God's fatherly relationship to the Son existed before creation, and the Son was never created. Even God's name "Father" suggests that the Son has always existed—if the Son did not always exist, to whom would God have been a Father?[4] The Father and Son have therefore existed together eternally (John 5:26), both equally God while also distinct as persons. Here already we are encountering the mysterious doctrine of the Trinity, to which we will later return.

---

[2] Romans 15:6; 2 Corinthians 1:3; Ephesians 1:3; Colossians 1:3; 1 Peter 1:3.

[3] John 1:3; see also Hebrews 1:3 and Colossians 1:16.

[4] Rufinus, *A Commentary on the Apostles' Creed*, 33–36.

Discussion

1. Read Psalm 148:4–5. How should we respond to the news that God is our creator?
2. An ancient false teaching (Arianism) claimed that Jesus was a created being, and some religions today teach the same (for example, Mormonism). Explain why this teaching is incorrect and why it matters. Read John 1:1–3 to help you answer.

Figure 3. Girona Tapestry from the eleventh century, housed in the Museum of the Cathedral of Girona, Catalonia, Spain. Christ the Almighty sits in the center of creation, with the Holy Spirit poised in the panel above him. The panels portray the seven days of creation. Image in the public domain, available in Wikimedia Commons.

Part 2

JESUS CHRIST

Session 4

I Believe in Jesus Christ, His Only Son, Our Lord

Now in the creed we come to the largest section. While the first and third sections of the creed teach about the Father and the Holy Spirit, the second section teaches at length about Jesus and his saving work.

The Hebrew form of Jesus' name, *Yeshua*, which was his true given name, means "Yahweh saves" (Yahweh being the name by which God revealed himself to his people in the Old Testament). So the first truth we learn about Jesus is that he is God in the flesh, who has come to save his people.[1] God promised throughout the Old Testament that

---

[1] As we will see, the Father and Son are distinct persons, but they are both equally God. When we say that Jesus is God in the flesh, we mean that the Son was born into this world as Jesus Christ, being both fully human and fully divine. The Father was not born into this world, but "sent" his Son to save the world (John 3:16; Galatians 4:4).

he would save his people from their sins, but no one expected that God himself would appear on earth as a man to do so!

The term "Christ" means "anointed one." In the Old Testament, priests or kings would be ceremonially anointed with oil to mark them as specially appointed by God for their task. "Christ" (or "Messiah," in Hebrew) eventually became the title for Israel's awaited Messiah who would save them from their sins.[2] "Christ" was therefore a title that could be applied to anyone who was anointed, such as Israel's king (Psalm 2:2), but eventually became a proper name, "Jesus Christ." We see that Jesus is greater than all previously anointed priests or kings, though. They were anointed with oil, but Christ was anointed with the Holy Spirit (Acts 10:38).[3]

Jesus Christ is the "Son of God," a title we have seen to refer to the second person of the Trinity. He stands in eternal relationship to his Father, equal in power and majesty. John's Gospel refers to Jesus as the Son of God in this sense most frequently, while the other Gospels do occasionally (see Matthew 11:25–27). But the term "son of God" is also used throughout the Bible to refer to a special relationship that other created beings have with God. These "sons" include Israel, a faithful portion of Israel, the Messiah, Israel's

---

[2] "Christ" comes from the Greek word *christos*, which is the Greek translation of the Hebrew word *māshîaḥ* ("Messiah"). So "Christ" and Messiah" are the same word in different languages, both meaning "anointed one."

[3] Rufinus, *A Commentary on the Apostles' Creed*, 39.

king, Adam, and angels.[4] When the first three Gospels refer to Jesus as the Son of God, they are essentially transferring the title "son" from unfaithful Israel and their king to the true King, Jesus Christ. While all other sons failed to live up to their calling, Jesus has perfectly obeyed the will of his Father, lived a sinless life, and represents the ideal of all that humanity was created to be. Want to know what it means to be truly human and to love God? Look to Jesus, the true Son of God.

Jesus is also "Lord." It is vital to understand what this title meant to those in Jesus' day. God identified himself to his people in the Old Testament by the Hebrew name "Yahweh." The Old Testament, written in ancient Hebrew, was translated into Greek by Jewish believers about 200 years before Jesus' day. In this Greek translation, the Hebrew name "Yahweh" was translated by the Greek word *Kurios*, which means "Lord." By Jesus' day, Greek was the common world language, which meant that the Greek Bible was widely used even by Jews. So God was known most frequently by his name in the Greek Bible, *Kurios*, "Lord." This means that when the Bible calls Jesus *Kurios*, "Lord," he bears God's own name! Jesus is the Son of God in the flesh. With this knowledge, we understand better the ancient confession from Romans 10:9: if you confess with your mouth that "Jesus is Lord" (God in the flesh), then you will be saved!

---

[4] Genesis 6:2–4; Exodus 4:22; Jeremiah 31:9; Hosea 11:1; Jeremiah 31:9; Hosea 1:10; Samuel 7:14; 1 Chronicles 17:13; 22:10; 28:6; Psalm 2:7; 89:26–27; Luke 3:38; Job 38:7.

Perhaps most surprising of all, Jesus is "our" Lord. He came to seek and to save the lost (Luke 19:10), and to be our shepherd—even our shepherd who would lay down his life for us (John 10:11). As the first question and answer of the Heidelberg Catechism puts it, "What is your only comfort in life and in death? That I, both body and soul, in life and in death, am not my own but belong to my faithful Savior Jesus Christ."[5]

Discussion

1. As a new follower of Jesus, who do you currently understand Jesus to be? Does your understanding need to change in order to align with the Bible's teaching about who he is?
2. In the past, who have you most admired and wanted to be like? If you instead admired and wanted to be like Jesus, what would you need to change in your life to become more like him?

---

[5] Noted by Cranfield, *The Apostles' Creed*, 25.

Figure 4. Jesus' choice to enter Jerusalem on a colt rather than a war horse signaled that he was redefining the concept of Messiah. Rather than coming to subdue the Romans to re-establish a physical kingdom, he was coming to serve and give his life as a ransom for many (Mark 10:45). He was establishing God's kingdom on earth through the power of the Spirit, not the sword. More than needing rescue from the Romans, Israel needed rescue from their sin. Image from the Nativity of the Theotokos Church in Bitola, Macedonia. Photo: Petar Milošević, CC BY-SA.

Session 5

Who Was Conceived by the Holy Spirit, Born of the Virgin Mary

The Bible teaches that "the birth of Jesus Christ took place in this way: when his mother Mary had been engaged to Joseph, before they came together she was found to be with child from the Holy Spirit" (Matthew 1:18). People have always found this teaching odd. By the second century, several popular false teachers were already claiming that Jesus was not born as a human by a virgin. But the virgin birth is actually significant because of the Bible's teaching on sin and how it would have affected Jesus had he been born normally.

When Adam and Eve—the first man and woman—were created, they were created free from sin. But, they had the capacity to sin if they chose it. Genesis 3 shows us that they willingly rebelled against God and brought sin into their lives and into the world. Among the many disastrous results of "the fall" (as we refer to this first sin and its effects) is that mankind acquired a sinful nature (Romans 5:19). Before the fall, Adam was theoretically capable of not sinning. But now, Adam and his children are forever tainted by sin and we are incapable of living a life free of sin.

Jesus came to undo the consequences of the fall. Whereas Adam brought sin and death into the world through his sin, Jesus brought "the free gift of righteousness" that Adam had lost (Romans 5:17). But in order to conquer sin and ensure that his followers could do the same, Jesus could not be born into a sinful nature. If he had been born naturally through Joseph and Mary, he would have acquired a sinful nature like every other son of Adam. His sinful nature inevitably would have caused him to sin, in which case he could not have been a sinless and spotless sacrifice for our sins. But because Jesus was conceived miraculously through the power of the Holy Spirit, he avoided inheriting this sinful nature and was able to lead a sinless life, despite being tempted in every way (Hebrews 4:15).

So also are we able to resist sin once God makes our hearts new. God works in us with the same power "that he worked in Christ when he raised him from the dead" (Ephesians 1:20). When we place our faith in Christ to save us from our sins, God sends us the Holy Spirit (Ephesians 1:14), the third person of the Trinity whom we will learn about later in the creed. Scripture tells us that we can put sin to death, but only if we do it by the power of the Spirit living in us (Romans 8:13). We see then that the virgin birth matters, because without it not only would Jesus have

Session 5

inherited a sinful nature at birth, but we would have been left with no way out of our own sin.

Discussion

1. Because of just *one sin*, all mankind inherited a sinful nature. What does this fact suggest about the power and danger of sin?
2. Read Romans 8:13. How do we overcome sin?

Figure 5. The Virgin with Child and Saint Anne, painted by Leonardo da Vinci. The infant Jesus grasps a sacrificial lamb, symbolizing his future sacrifice as the "lamb of God that takes away the sin of the world" (John 1:29), as Mary tries to restrain him. Image in the public domain, available in Wikimedia Commons.

Session 6

Suffered under Pontius Pilate

The creed is silent on Jesus' life, moving straight from his virgin birth to his death. This omission is probably the creed's greatest flaw (or oversight). One of the merits of the creed, however, is that it situates our Christian faith in time and space. Pontius Pilate was the Roman governor of Judea from AD 26–36. He spoke to the mob who wanted to crucify Jesus and finally gave in to their demand. This historical account can be found in Luke 23.

That the Christian faith is based on historical events is what distinguishes it from most other major world religions (e.g., Hinduism and Buddhism). Christianity is not based on philosophical principles or wisdom gathered from human experience, like the sayings attributed to Confucius. Such sayings are only the earthly wisdom of human beings. Rather, Christianity is based on something that happened in time and space and was witnessed by hundreds of people (1 Corinthians 15:6), some of whom wrote down what they saw (which is how we got the Gospels; see Luke 1:1–4). No other religion claims that God became a human, was tried under a worldly ruler, was killed by men, and later rose from his own grave to prove his divinity. Other religions, like Islam, base their beliefs on prophets who never claimed to be God, never performed miracles, and never rose from the dead.

While the creed focuses only on the suffering under Pilate when Jesus was tried and crucified, we can expand that focus to consider the sufferings of Jesus' entire life. He willingly took on flesh to enter his own creation and gave up his divine rights and powers for the sake of living a genuine human life in order to redeem and restore mankind (Philippians 2:6–7). The suffering of Christ in the entire history of his life offers us a true measure of the depth of our sin.[1] Just as we learn about the severity of a disease by learning of the extremity of its cure, so also we learn of the severity of our sin by learning that its cure was the rejection and crucifixion of the Creator's Son at the hands of his own creatures.

It also follows that, if we serve the one who suffered to such an extent, we too shall suffer with him. Jesus promised, "If they persecuted me, they will also persecute you" (John 15:20). And yet our often-tragic suffering works through the sovereignty of God for the good of our witness. "We are afflicted in every way, but not crushed; perplexed, but not driven to despair; persecuted, but not forsaken;

---

[1] Brooke Foss Westcott, *The Historic Faith: Short Lectures on the Apostles' Creed*, 3rd ed. (Macmillan & Co., 1885), 68.

struck down, but not destroyed; always carrying in the body the death of Jesus, so that the life of Jesus may also be manifested in our bodies" (2 Corinthians 4:8–10). Our suffering (if it is for the sake of righteousness) is a witness to the world of the same suffering that Jesus endured, and is therefore an extension of his earthly ministry to this broken world.

Discussion

1. Read Luke 1:1–4 and 1 Corinthians 15:6. Why does it matter that the Bible is based on human testimony to historical events such as Jesus' resurrection?
2. Are you willing to follow Jesus' path of suffering as his disciple? If so, what do you think it might mean in your life for people to "persecute you" (John 15:20)?

Figure 6. Jesus (left), wearing a crown of thorns, stands trial before Pontius Pilate (right), who resigns himself to delivering Jesus to the Jewish leaders to be crucified. The sculpture is part of the Passion Façade of the Temple of the Sagrada Família in Barcelona. Josep Maria Subirachs sculpted the scene based on the design of Antoni Gaudí. Construction on the entire Passion Façade began in 1954 and was completed in 2018. Image in the public domain, available in Wikimedia Commons.

Session 7

Was Crucified, Died, and Was Buried; He Descended to the Dead

Crucifixion was one of the worst forms of death ever invented by man. It was used occasionally by some ancient societies, but the Romans perfected it. Typical Jews and Romans detested crucifixion because it was considered an accursed slave's death.[1] The victim would carry the horizontal beam of the cross to his own place of execution. His arms would then be nailed or bound to this beam, which would be attached to the vertical beam, to which the victim's feet would be nailed. The victim would hang on the cross for days in agony before dying. Jesus had been beaten so severely before his crucifixion that he was not even able to carry the horizontal beam of his cross to the site of his death (Mark 15:21). The excruciating nature of our Savior's death calls us to humbly praise him for subjecting himself to such torture at the hands of his own creatures.

---

[1] Deuteronomy 21:23; Cicero, *Pro Rabirio* 5.

There are several reasons why Jesus came to die. First, Adam and Eve (the first created human couple) failed to fulfill God's intention for humanity. They had been commissioned to rule over creation as God's "image" and fill the earth with children who would do the same (Genesis 1:26–28). Their rule would represent God's rule as they reflected who God is. Christ came as the ideal man, the true "*image* of the invisible God" (Colossians 1:15). Through his resurrection, he was seated at the right hand of God (a place of power) from where he rules over all creation as Adam was supposed to (Ephesians 1:20–22; Hebrews 2:8–9). As we place our faith in Christ and follow him, we enter into the Kingdom of God and participate with Christ in reflecting to the nations God's rule over his creation.

A second reason Jesus came to die was to deal with sin. We, as God's image on earth, became imperfect and flawed through sin. The New Testament is clear that Adam's sin set the entire course of humanity on a downward spiral. Through Adam's sin, "many died" (Romans 5:15), meaning that Adam's sin caused all his descendants to inherit the spiritually dead nature of their first father. Adam's sin "led to condemnation for all men" (Romans 5:18) because through Adam's "disobedience the many were made sinners" (Romans 5:19). In other words, humanity's moral capacities were tainted. Our nature became sinful so that we are born as "children of wrath" (Ephesians 2:3) and "enemies" of God (Romans 5:10). Jesus took on "the likeness of sinful flesh" in order to "condemn sin in the flesh" (Romans 8:3). His resistance to sin proved that he had power over it, and therefore that he has the ability to remove it from us and even to declare us "righteous" before God.

But how could we be "righteous" when we still sin? Because we are not made sinless through faith; rather, we are credited Christ's righteousness as if it were our own. "For our sake, he made him to be sin who knew no sin, so that *in him* we might become the righteousness of God" (2 Corinthians 5:21). By "in him," Scripture refers to our intimate relationship with Christ through faith. It is through this relationship that we receive all of our saving benefits and blessings from God.

This sin that Christ came to deal with had a more severe consequence than we often care to think about—it incurred and deserved the wrath of God.[2] God is just; he is not one to sweep sin under the rug and allow gross injustices against his beloved people without recompense. All people who have sinned and earned death (Romans 6:23) are subject to the wrath of God, but God sent Jesus to deal with our sin so we could have a way to escape his wrath and be reconciled to him.

There are many other reasons Jesus came to die. One book pulls from the Bible fifty different reasons![3] To list only a few, Jesus came to die to please his Father (Isaiah 53:10), to show God's love for sinners (Romans 5:7–8; John 3:16), to make us holy and complete (Colossians 1:22), to give us a clean conscience (Hebrews 9:14), to give us access

---

[2] Romans 1:18; 2:5; 1 Thessalonians 2:15–16; Ephesians 5:6; Colossians 3:6.

[3] John Piper, *Fifty Reasons Why Jesus Came to Die* (Wheaton, IL: Crossway, 2006).

to a holy God (Ephesians 2:18), to give us an example of selflessness (1 Peter 2:21; Philippians 2:5–11), to subdue the evil spiritual forces (Colossians 2:15), and so that we would live for Christ (2 Corinthians 5:15). Ultimately, these problems all started when Adam and Eve introduced sin into the world. This rebellion distorted God's intention for humanity and tainted humanity with a sinful nature. Jesus came to die to fix all that.

The burial of Christ is significant for two reasons. First, it testifies against an ancient false teaching (Docetism) that claimed that Jesus came as a spirit, not as an actual human being. We know that spirits are not buried. His burial is therefore a three-day reminder that the God of the universe took on real human flesh to save his people. Second, his death is symbolic of the death of our old selves, our old lifestyles that we repent of and pledge to leave behind when we give our allegiance to Christ. "We were buried with him by baptism into death, in order that, just as Christ was raised from the dead by the glory of the Father, we too might walk in newness of life" (Romans 6:4). So our baptism is a way in which we identify with Christ in both his death and resurrection. Our old self is dead, and our new self has risen from the spiritual grave, following in Jesus' path.[4]

---

[4] The meaning and significance of baptism is understood differently by various theological traditions. Some traditions hold that only those who profess faith in Christ should be baptized, while other traditions baptize the babies of Christian families in order to include the entire family in the covenant community. Consult with your pastor to discuss the meaning and significance

The phrase "he descended to the dead" is taken directly from Ephesians 4:9, which says Jesus "descended into the lowest parts of the earth."[5] This region is often understood as "hell," but Ephesians 4:9 is not so specific. A more accurate interpretation of this statement is that Jesus descended to the place of the dead. Why does the creed include this belief? According to Ephesians 4:9–10, Jesus descended into the lowest parts of creation and then, after his resurrection, ascended "far above the heavens" to take his place of honor and power at the right hand of God (Ephesians 1:20). He did this "in order to fill all things" with his power and sovereignty (Ephesians 4:10). In other words, he visited every corner of creation, including the place of the dead, and conquered it. Jesus has expressed his complete control and power over the entire universe that he shares with his Father. If we belong to Jesus, whom or what shall we fear?

Discussion

1. Read Romans 6:23 and Romans 2:5. What do these verses say about the consequences of sin?
2. What are three reasons Jesus came to die by crucifixion? Which of these is most significant to you, and why?

---

of baptism in your tradition and to answer any questions you may have.

[5] The Greek text of the creed is almost exactly the same as Ephesians 4:9, so the creed could be translated literally as "having descended into the lowest parts." I have translated it as "to the dead" since the interpretation given here equates "the lower parts" with the realm of the dead.

3. Read Romans 5:6–10. How does Jesus deal with our sin and save us from the wrath of God?

Figure 7. A portrait of Jesus' death and descent to the dead, painted around AD 1500. Image in the public domain, available in Wikimedia Commons.

Session 8

On the Third Day, He Rose Again; He Ascended into Heaven, He is Sitting at the Right Hand of God the Father Almighty

Jesus predicted at least three times that he would die and rise again: "the Son of Man (Jesus) must suffer many things and be rejected by the elders and the chief priests and the scribes and be killed, and after three days rise again" (Mark 8:31; see also Mark 9:31; 10:33–34). This prediction was known even to the Jewish leaders after his death, who wanted to prevent his disciples from stealing Jesus' body from the tomb to fake his resurrection (Matthew 27:63–66). Despite these increased security measures, when the women who loved Jesus came to honor him at his grave, the large stone that sat in front of his tomb had been rolled away, and Jesus was not there (Luke 24:1–3). Jesus had descended into the realm of the dead for three days and then conquered the grave, defeated death, and proved that he is truly God in the flesh with power over all creation.

Jesus' resurrection was not simply a resuscitation of his old body, but the creation of a *new* resurrection body. The Old Testament prophesied that God would recreate the heavens and the earth, which had been tainted and corrupted by sin: "For behold, I create new heavens and a new earth, and the former things shall not be remembered or come into mind" (Isaiah 65:17). This promise includes the recreation of human bodies, which would be eternally fit for the new creation. Jesus' new resurrection body was the first act of new creation in this old world. His body was barely recognizable by his own disciples (John 20:15; 21:4; Luke 24:16). It was made "imperishable," one fit for eternity (1 Corinthians 15:42).

That Jesus' resurrection was the initial phase of the new creation is stated in a beautiful poem in the letter to the Colossians. Christ is "the beginning," that is, the beginning of the new creation that God had promised (Colossians 1:18). If he is the "beginning," there is more to come. His resurrection paved the way for *our* resurrection! "Christ has been raised from the dead, the firstfruits of those who have fallen asleep....in Christ all will be made alive. But each in his own order: Christ the firstfruits, then at his coming those who belong to Christ" (1 Corinthians 15:20, 22–23). His resurrection holds out two promises. First, God will complete this work of recreating the heavens and earth that he promised. Second, when Christ returns, God will resurrect his followers to receive their new imperishable resurrection bodies, fit to live in the new creation with God for eternity.

After Jesus's resurrection, he ascended into heaven, where he "sat down" at the "right hand of God the Father." In the ancient world, the "right hand" was symbolic of a place of power and authority. His ascension to God's right hand demonstrates his equality with God's nature and power; it also fulfilled Scripture. Psalm 110:1 prophesied about a future "Lord" who would sit at God's right hand and rule over all of God's enemies. Jesus found this prophecy so important that he identified himself as the "Lord" of which the psalm spoke (Mark 12:35–37). This prophecy is also cited in the New Testament more than any other Old Testament text, which is why the idea of Christ's ascension to God's right hand made its way into the creed.[1] Jesus put all of God's enemies under his feet at the cross, where evil was subdued (Colossians 2:15). But the final destruction of evil awaits the future judgment (Revelation 19:20–21). While we await that judgment, we can know that Christ is at the right hand of God, in supreme control and authority over all evil and rebellious spiritual beings.

Discussion

1. Read 1 Corinthians 15:20–23. Why is it important that Christ received a resurrection body instead of simply having his old body resuscitated?
2. Read 2 Peter 3:13. Where will we spend eternity with God?

---

[1] Acts 2:34; Romans 8:34; 1 Corinthians 15:25; Ephesians 1:20; Colossians 3:1; Hebrews 1:3; 1:13; 8:1; 10:12; 12:2; 1 Peter 3:22.

3. Since Christ is at the right hand of God, how should we respond to tragedy, misfortune, and evil in our lives?

Figure 8. Sixteenth century Renaissance artist Garofalo portrays Christ ascending into heaven. Image in the public domain, available in Wikimedia Commons.

Session 9

From Where He is Coming to Judge the Living and the Dead

Jesus' resurrection was not the final act of God for his people. The Old Testament consistently testifies that God will come in the future to judge humanity.[1] The New Testament clarifies that it will be Christ (God the Son) who will come on the Day of the Lord (1 Thessalonians 4:16) to judge humanity (Matthew 25:31–34). Those who have trusted in Christ for salvation will be welcomed into his kingdom: "Come, you who are blessed by my Father, inherit the kingdom prepared for you from the foundation of the world" (Matthew 25:34). Those who have rejected salvation in Christ will remain in their sin and face the wrath of God.

---

[1] Isaiah 13:6, 9; Jeremiah 46:10; Ezekiel 30:3; Joel 1:15; 2:1; 2:11; 2:31; 3:14; 5:18; 5:20; Obadiah 15; Zephaniah 1:7, 14; Malachi 4:5; 1 Corinthians 5:5; 1 Thessalonians 5:2; 2 Thessalonians 2:2; 2 Peter 3:10.

Christ the Judge will declare to them, "Depart from me, you cursed, into the eternal fire prepared for the devil and his angels" (Matthew 25:41).

Passages of Scripture that mention the Day of the Lord also direct us to live with the future judgment in mind. "Be diligent to be found by him without spot or blemish, and at peace" (2 Peter 3:14). "Encourage one another and build one another up" (1 Thessalonians 5:11). "Rejoice always, pray without ceasing; give thanks in all circumstances; for this is the will of God in Christ Jesus for you. Do not quench the Spirit. Do not despise prophecies, but test everything. Hold fast what is good. Abstain from every form of evil. Now may the God of peace himself sanctify you completely, and may your whole spirit and soul and body be kept blameless at the coming of our Lord Jesus Christ" (1 Thessalonians 5:16–23).

Our actions are important not because they are the basis on which we are saved—we have already seen that we are saved on the basis of our faith (Ephesians 2:8–9; Galatians 2:16). Our actions are important because true disciples will have new hearts and the Spirit will direct them to walk in the commandments of the Lord (Ezekiel 36:26–27). This means that *part* of our assurance that we are truly saved is that we are walking in new ways and are eager to serve and love the Lord. If we remember Jesus is coming soon to judge the living and the dead, we will be all the more eager to ensure that our lives are testifying to the genuineness of our faith.

Session 9 45

Discussion

1. Since you've placed your faith in Christ, how have you seen evidence that you have a new heart and that the Spirit is guiding you to walk in God's commandments?
2. Read Galatians 2:16. What is the basis on which we are saved?
3. Read Matthew 25:34–40. What is the role of our works (our actions) in the future judgment? How do they act as a testimony for or against us? (Keep in mind they are not the basis on which we are saved.)

Figure 9. This masterpiece occupied Italian Renaissance painter Michelangelo from AD 1536–1541. Covering the entire altar wall of the Sistine Chapel in Vatican City, it depicts the final day of judgment, when those who have trusted in Christ for salvation will be welcomed into his kingdom. Image in the public domain, available in Wikimedia Commons.

Part 3

THE GIFTS OF GOD

Session 10

I Believe in the Holy Spirit

The third section of the creed begins by proclaiming belief in the third person of the Trinity, the Holy Spirit. God's Spirit, like the Son, was involved in creation (Genesis 1:2) and therefore has existed eternally with the Father and Son. The Spirit is a distinct person from the Father and Son but exists as God. The Spirit's divinity is clear in Acts 5, for example. A married couple lied to the church about their financial contribution, to which Peter replied, "Ananias, why has Satan filled your heart to lie to the Holy Spirit and to keep back for yourself part of the proceeds of the land?" (Acts 5:3). Only a few sentences later, Peter reiterates, "You have not lied to man but to God" (Acts 5:4). Scripture presents the Holy Spirit as God, equal in majesty and authority to the Father and Son.

The Trinity is perhaps the greatest mystery we can encounter. That three persons could simultaneously have the attributes of "God" (e.g., being all-powerful) is hard to fathom. But Scripture is consistent throughout that God is one (Deuteronomy 6:4) and that three persons are God. Despite the popularity of using metaphors from creation to explain the Trinity (three-leafed clovers, the three states of water, etc.), all metaphors fall short. We must settle with this truth that seems to be a mystery, and which only God can truly comprehend: there is one God, and God is three persons.

This chapter is entitled "The Gifts of God" because, despite the seemingly random nature of the final lines of the creed, they might all be considered together as the gifts of God. The Holy Spirit is Christ's gift to the church (Acts 2:38; Ephesians 4:7). He is given to those who place their faith in Christ as a "down payment" their inheritance (Ephesians 1:13–14). Although we still remain in this old world, the Holy Spirit is the presence of God within us, which stands as a promise that we will be given "our inheritance," our place in the new creation.

As the Holy Spirit fills us and empowers us (Ephesians 5:18), we are enabled to obey God's commandments (according to the prophecy in Ezekiel 36:26–27). Through the Holy Spirit, we can put to death the sin that remains in us (Romans 8:13). If we are led by the Spirit of God, then we have evidence that we are truly the sons of God (Romans 8:14–17). The Spirit helps us pray in spite of our weakness (Romans 8:26). The Spirit is also the one who convicts "the world concerning sin and righteousness and judgment" (John 16:8). We must acknowledge that it was the Spirit of God that overcame our sinful hearts to enable us to believe the gospel, and we must pray that he would do the same to those with whom we share the gospel.

Discussion

1. How many persons are simultaneously God? Are you comfortable with this mystery? Why or why not?
2. Based on what is explained above, what are three things the Spirit does for us?
3. Read John 16:8. Whose role is it to convict others of their sin? What is the difference between convicting someone of their sin and sharing with someone that they are a sinner in need of a savior.

Figure 10. El Bautismo de Jesús, by Brazilian artist José Ferraz De Almeida Júnior, painted in 1895. At Jesus' baptism, the Holy Spirit descended on Jesus like a dove, and the Father spoke from heaven, "You are my beloved Son; with you I am well pleased" (Mark 1:11). In this scene, the Triune God is fully present: Father, Son, and Holy Spirit. Image in the public domain, available in Wikimedia Commons.

Session 11

The Holy Universal Church, The Communion of Saints

The church is a gift of God to the world. The word "church" is translated in our Bibles from words in the Old and New Testaments that actually mean "assembly." But the church is not just any assembly. In the Old Testament, Israel was the "assembly *of the Lord.*" So when Jesus referred to his people as an "assembly" (or "church," as we translate it) he meant specifically that his people are the "assembly of the Lord," gathered before him in worship. The church is therefore the assembly of those who follow and worship the Lord together.

The church is the only institution Jesus left in this world. He built the church on the foundation of Peter (Matthew 16:18)—but only Peter insofar as he represented all the apostles as the ideal confessor of the true identity of Christ. "You are Christ, the Son of the Living God," Peter confessed (Matthew 16:16). The church is therefore "built on the foundation of the apostles" (Ephesians 2:20), who acted as the mouthpiece of Christ on earth after his ascension.[1] If the church is founded on the apostles, and the apostles authored Scripture by the inspiration of the Holy Spirit, then everything that the church does and proclaims must be based on the apostolic word found in the Scriptures.

The church is "universal," that is, worldwide. While millions of communities of believers gather together each Sunday, there is only one worldwide church, established by Jesus Christ, composed of all true believers. As believers in Christ we are "saints" (holy ones), cleansed of our sin and prepared for God's special use in this world. Our "communion" (meeting together) is important. We are to "stir up one another to love and good works, not neglecting to meet together...but encouraging one another, and all the more as you see the Day [of the Lord's return] drawing near" (Hebrews 10:24–25). Christians cannot hate or neglect the church, because it is Christ's bride (Revelation 21:9), and because it is the most important means of being encouraged in our faith.

The church must be a witness to the world of the gospel of Jesus Christ (Matthew 28:19–20). We carry out this mission to the world together, all adopted into the same spiritual family, which is known to the world by our love for one another (1 John 3:14; John 13:35). Each of us has a part to play in order for the church to grow in love. Each believ-

---

[1] The apostles are those who saw Jesus after his resurrection and whom Jesus sent to preach the gospel around the world.

er has been given certain spiritual gifts. To the extent that each believer uses these gifts properly, the church "builds itself up in love" (Ephesians 4:7; 4:16). We are called to work diligently to build up the church, so it will become unified and mature in Christ (Colossians 1:28; Ephesians 4:13).

Discussion

1. Based on the reading above, define "church" in one sentence.
2. According to Matthew 28:19–20, what is the church's mission to the world?
3. According to Hebrews 10:24–25, why is it important for believers to consistently and continually meet together?

Figure 11. The remains of an ancient building where a third century Syrian congregation met for worship. It was typical in the earliest centuries of the church for local believers to meet in the homes of wealthy individuals. This building was one such "house church," but it was donated to the congregation around AD 240 and converted for more permanent use.[2] They removed one wall to create a larger worship and prayer area, and added a baptistery. The walls of the baptistery were painted with Christian themes, including the healing of the paralytic that is pictured above in Figure 2 on page 11. Whether the meeting place was an individual's home, or a building devoted for worship, it was still the followers of Jesus who were the church, the "assembly of the Lord."

---

[2] For more information and images, see the interactive webpage by Yale University, http://media.artgallery.yale.edu/duraeuropos (last accessed September 28, 2019).

Session 12

The Forgiveness of Sins, The Resurrection of the Body, And the Life Everlasting

The final gifts we receive are those that we have already come across. Jesus' death was the sacrifice we needed for the forgiveness of our sins. In the Old Testament, God required animal sacrifices for the forgiveness of sins. These sacrifices were God's way of providing the Israelites a substitute to receive the punishment they deserved for their sin. The animal's owner would symbolically transfer their guilt to the animal, which would then be killed as the owner's substitute (Leviticus 1:4).

But as the New Testament teaches, animal sacrifices were a temporary setup. Animal sacrifice brought neither permanent forgiveness nor sufficient forgiveness, for "it is impossible for the blood of bulls and goats to take away sins" (Hebrews 10:4). The death of animals could not truly make up for the damage done to God's good creation through the sins of mankind.

To obtain the permanent forgiveness of sins, God sent his Son to be the spotless "Lamb of God who takes away the sin of the world" by his sacrificial death (John 1:29). Not only was Jesus' death sufficient to cover all sins, but it also dealt with all sins permanently on the cross. "He has appeared once for all at the end of the ages to put away sin by the sacrifice of himself" (Hebrews 9:26). Our eternal forgiveness secures our eternal relationship with our creator. We were "enemies of God," but now we have been "reconciled to God by the death of his Son" (Romans 5:10).

The resurrection of our bodies will occur similarly to the resurrection of Jesus' body. It will not be a resuscitation of our old bodies. At Jesus' return, his followers will receive their resurrection bodies, fit for the recreated world. Just as God was present among his people in the Garden of Eden (Genesis 3:8–9), so he will be eternally present with his people in the new creation (Revelation 21:1–3). In the new creation, God "will wipe away every tear from their eyes, and death shall be no more, neither shall there be mourning, nor crying, nor pain anymore, for the former things have passed away" (Revelation 21:4).

It is only because we receive these resurrection bodies, and because God banishes death from the new creation, that we can experience "life everlasting." "Everlasting" not only describes the duration of our life but also the *quality* of life. Living forever would be torment if the quality of life were not one worth having forever. Life everlasting is life that is indestructible, imperishable, full of unending joy, and lacking anything that would leave us wanting more.

Life everlasting is full of the most gracious gifts that God can give his people. He is far more gracious, creative, and fulfilling than we could ever imagine or hope, so we should not presume that we will ever become bored in the new creation. Of course, the greatest of all gifts is the presence of the Triune God. We will never cease to satisfy ourselves with the unending joy that comes from the full and unmediated presence of the Father, Son, and Holy Spirit.

Discussion

1. According to Hebrews 9:22, what is required in order for God to forgive sins? Who provided that requirement so that our sins could be forgiven?
2. The creed says we believe in "life everlasting." What is the difference between living forever and having a quality of life that makes someone want to live forever?
3. According to the reading above, what is the greatest of all gifts we will receive after the resurrection? Why is it the greatest gift we could receive?

Figure 12. Based on the book of Revelation, this eleventh century painting symbolically portrays the New Jerusalem. The Father sits on his throne with the Book of Life in his hand and the Son at his feet as the lamb. The trees on both sides of the Father and Son symbolize the New Jerusalem as Eden restored. Image in the public domain, available in Wikimedia Commons.

Next Steps

Beginning to Grow in the Faith

In 2 Corinthians 13:5, Paul tells the Corinthians to "examine yourselves, to see whether you are in the faith. Test yourselves." This guide has been an attempt to allow you the opportunity to examine yourself. While the confession that "Jesus is Lord" that must be on the lips of all believers, we must make this confession with a proper understanding of its meaning. We have examined the core beliefs of the Christian faith pertaining to the Father, the Son, and the gifts of God to his people. If you now understand these beliefs and hold to them, then you have a firm foundation to grow in your relationship with Jesus Christ. That is the sole purpose of this guide.

But biblical faith is not as simple as believing something is true. If we stop there, we fall prey to James' warning that "faith without works is dead" (James 2:26). Jesus' call to repent is a call to turn from sin and toward Jesus. Faith in its fullness is our wholehearted devotion to Jesus

Christ *because* we believe what the Scriptures say about him. Therefore, while this guide is a solid foundation, discipleship does not stop here. This study has only been the beginning. There are several ways to continue growing in your faith and many resources to help you.

Church Membership

One of the most important steps for your discipleship is to find a church to belong to. We are commanded not to skip out on meeting regularly with our fellow believers (Hebrews 10:24–25). Church leaders are obligated to care for the souls of a specific group of believers, and those believers are to submit to their leaders for spiritual guidance and care: "Obey your leaders and submit to them, for they are keeping watch over your souls, as those who will have to give an account" (Hebrews 13:17). It follows that every disciple of Christ should join a local church if possible so they can be under the spiritual care of the church's leaders.

Spiritual Disciplines

Being a disciple of Christ means to have a daily relationship with him as Lord, Master, and Teacher. There are a variety of spiritual disciplines that help you connect with the Triune God. While you might not practice each one every day, they are all important to a vibrant and growing faith. The most common spiritual disciplines are Scripture reading, prayer, worship, evangelism, serving, stewardship of personal finances (including tithing), fasting, silence and meditation, journaling, and learning. These disciplines are all discussed and illustrated in Donald Whitney's *Spiritual Disciplines for the Christian Life*, rev. ed. (NavPress, 2014). I recommend this book because it emphasizes the importance of spiritual disciplines and motivates you to practice them. If you prefer to learn about the spiritual disciplines in an engaging narrative form, try John Linebarger's *Meeting God in the Bible: How to Read Scripture Devotionally* (Fontes, 2019). You should have consistent opportunities to practice many of these disciplines in your local church, while some require intentional time alone throughout the week.

BIBLICAL KNOWLEDGE

We can only learn more about our Savior through the Scriptures. The Apostles' Creed outlines the basic elements of the Christian faith, but the riches of the Bible are endless. "Oh, the depth of the riches and wisdom and knowledge of God! How unsearchable are his judgments and how inscrutable his ways!" (Romans 11:33). The more we understand the Bible and can apply it rightly to our lives, the closer we will walk with the Lord.

There are two ways to study the Bible. The first approach is the one taken in this guide, which is to teach about important beliefs from the Bible arranged by topic. For this approach, I recommend as your next resource Wayne Grudem's *Christian Beliefs: Twenty Basics Every Christian Should Know* (Zondervan, 2005). The second approach to studying the Bible is to try to grasp it as an entire story of God's saving work from the creation of the world in Genesis to the recreation of the heavens and the earth in Revelation. For this approach, I recommend Tim Chester's *From Creation to New Creation: Making Sense of the Whole Bible Story* (The Good Book Company, 2010). For a more informative but also a more challenging book, I recommend D. A. Carson's *The God Who is There: Finding Your Place in God's Story* (Baker, 2010).

Some parts of the Bible are straightforward and easy to apply, but other parts are difficult and obscure. This difficulty stems from the fact that it was written by dozens of authors over a period of 1,500 years. Even biblical scholars still need help interpreting the Bible! A popular book that will help you start overcoming these difficulties is Gordon Fee's and Douglas Stuart's *How to Read the Bible for All Its Worth*, 4th ed. (Zondervan, 2014). Investing time in reading this book will enrich your Scripture reading for years to come.

Online resources for studying the Bible are abounding. At BiblicalTraining.org, you can find courses and seminars from a very basic level to an advanced graduate level. The classes are provided by senior scholars and pastors whose work can be trusted. On the other hand, using Google or YouTube to search for topics is risky. You are likely to find yourself reading biased information from non-specialists whose work cannot be wholly trusted. While the resources are plentiful, you should be careful with the sources you trust. Consult with your pastor or church leaders for further trustworthy sources.

Biblical knowledge is priceless, but unless you know how to follow Christ in today's world you will feel dead in your faith. There are hundreds of Christian classics from which you would profit by reading, but there are a few works that have been especially influential for the modern Western church. John Piper's *Desiring God: Meditations of a Christian Hedonist*, rev. ed. (Multnomah, 2011) has convinced a generation to pursue their own joy and satisfaction in Christ *because* that most glorifies God (so he argues). Tim Keller's *The Reason for God: Belief in an Age of Skepticism* (Penguin, 2008) is a biblical and intellectual response to modern disbelief in God and the Christian faith. Larry Moyer's tiny *How-To Book on Personal Evangelism* (Kregel, 1998) is an excellent guide to using the right language and strategy for sharing the gospel effectively. These books will get you started as a life-long disciple of Christ. Once you've finished these, your pastor or church leaders should be more than happy to direct you to further resources.

www.ingramcontent.com/pod-product-compliance
Lightning Source LLC
Chambersburg PA
CBHW050333120526
44592CB00014B/2162